*A sweet, compelling short story for real dog lovers.*

*A one-sitting read, which most will relate.*

Betty, the protagonist, is a beautiful basset hound. Her posse is composed of Hootie, Boogie, and Hummel, her pups who were accidentally chemically enhanced during her pregnancy. This is the story of the joy of raising these unique characters and the friends that came into their lives.

# Betty

## and the Posse

# Betty

## and the Posse

By Jeremy Garton, PhD

Order this book online at www.trafford.com
or email orders@trafford.com

Most Trafford titles are also available at major online book retailers.

Printed in Victoria, BC, Canada.

ISBN: 978-1-4269-2818-5

Library of Congress Control Number: 2010904062

*Our mission is to efficiently provide the world's finest, most comprehensive book publishing
service, enabling every author to experience success. To find out how to publish your
book, your way, and have it available worldwide, visit us online at www.trafford.com*

*Trafford rev. 3/23/2010*

**Trafford** PUBLISHING®  www.trafford.com

**North America & international**
toll-free: 1 888 232 4444 (USA & Canada)
phone: 250 383 6864 ♦ fax: 812 355 4082

# A Special Acknowledgment:

A special acknowledgment has to go to the Acres North Animal Hospital staff and Dr. Kyle Crowley for his ability to maintain strength for people in their darkest hours. All of you are a godsend.

Thanks also to Tanya Baker—such a delicate and warm creature—her love of Prissy was so reassuring. The sight of them running down the beach together will hopefully be one of my last thoughts.

# Chapter 1

## First Meeting

It was strange to discover that I could fall totally in love in the twilight of my life. There were many before her, and I thought I had loved them. I now know total, unequivocal love. The other loves were a good sounding board or reference, but they were only pretenders to my heart—and my love.

It would be an injustice to try to describe her with mere earthly adjectives; she is, and will be, so much more. See, she is so beautiful in heart, mind, soul, and body; there are so many dimensions to her that I discover daily. Everything you associate with the concept of good and wonderful is embodied in Betty.

When I first met her, she was with someone .Her cool demeanor and aloofness left me thinking she was a snob. Besides, at the time, I also had another. Over time, I started gradually to discover her charms, and it took no time for her to win my heart.

Perfect entities do perfect things. In a way, I would prefer Betty not be perfect. That way, I would feel more deserving. But she loves me anyway.

With all my foibles, personality quirks, warts, and blemishes, she sees past all my faults and loves me, she could not love me more.

There are some drawbacks to a love so strong, so unfettered, and by convention, so totally open. The stronger the love, the harder the loss, I know. My fear is losing Betty. In many cases, one would withhold something of one's soul and passion, so the hurt of loss would not be so immense. You cannot do this with Betty. You just cannot love her enough and certainly cannot withhold anything, because she is so disarming. You scrape your very essences to find more to give.

There are things Betty does that are so endearing one cannot help but smile—like the way she brings her bowl when it is feeding time but refuses to eat from it. This is her tool to tell me to get up and get cooking. You have to have a gentle, caring nature about yourself, with time to devote. If you are fortunate enough, you too will see your dog as I portray my Betty. First, you have to be capable of an immense love, one that goes deep into the recesses of your heart and soul. That's where this special love lives. The rest is up to the Betty's of the world. They provide an introduction to what heaven must be like.

You know, as I'm writing this book, I have a big smile on my face. There are so many things Betty does for me. I cannot find the words to describe how I feel; they are fleeting feelings that engulf my being, and I feel warmth and love. At other times, she is so steadfast in her love, you know she will protect, stand by, and even die for you.

Betty communicates with me. I have not taught her demeaning tricks, humanizing her. Far from that, I have learned how to speak dog, and now, I am bilingual. Of course, she has mastered my language, though she refuses to use it. She understands but prefers her native tongue. She has a heightened sense and awareness of my feelings, which no human has.

Dogs and animals in general, are on loan to us by a higher entity. They enter our lives; they truly come in peace. They are here to remind us of compassion and love.

Yes, this is a dog book, so if you do not care about dogs, then shut this book and go to another section of the bookstore where you belong. If you are still reading, then you understand. See if your dog compares to Betty. No, Betty does not die in the book.

# Chapter 2

## Her Adoption

Betty was a full-blooded three-year-old basset hound, who adopted us. She came to us from the abused families program. We were her rescue family, opposed to a rescue dog. She was dubious at first we were not well trained and did not have a distinguished past with animals. We were fortunate that she adopted us. Betty had certain conditions to be met before she would adopt us. One was that we had to have a reputable veterinarian. She had to interview us before we could proceed, and she needed to get vaccinations for all the diseases humans carry.

We almost messed up our relationship from the start. We picked her up at the resort (kennel) and took her directly to the vet. She had contracted heartworms. To this day, I blame it on my sister (the other half of this ownership). Susan is a physician, so she probably had more exposure than I; besides, she kisses every dog she meets on the mouth. We had to leave Betty with the vet for a month to get rid of the worms. They had to inject her with a chemical to kill the worms, and in all seriousness, it could have killed her.

This was a precursor of what was to come. When we would go to the vet to visit Betty, all the employees were walking around with these smiles on their faces, just talking about Betty. Knowing they saw thousands of dogs in a year, I thought this overboard, but they would support their enthusiasm by recounting an event involving Betty. They promoted Betty to the front desk. She was the vet's emissary. She had a calming effect on animals that were frightened, and she was approachable to all the animals' human pets. She would follow the doctors to their rooms, as if escorting them, and then, once she had seen the patient, she would leave.

# Chapter 3

## Betty's Surprise

Bassets are a full-bodied breed, but Betty was thin when we left her at the vet's. Two weeks into her month-long stay, the vet noticed she was gaining more weight than expected. She had become rotund. We expected during a month at the vet's that she would gain some weight, but we had not expected this exponential gain. The vet performed x-rays, an ultrasound, and a sonogram. They discovered Betty was pregnant. As matter of fact, she was past the halfway point of the pregnancy, and from what we could tell, the fetuses were viable.

We wondered if the chemical which Betty had been injected for a month would have a profound effect on the puppies. The vet told us they had researched the situation and could not find where this had occurred before. Our natural inclination was to abort the babies, but we decided to let nature take its course. They might be born dead. Hopefully, there would be no four-eyed, eight-legged ones. What we got was little chemically altered miracles.

Of course, it all had to happen in the middle of the night. My sister woke me to tell me Betty was in distress; she would not settle and was dropping dead babies all over the house and yard. Susie tried to settle Betty as I gathered her dead babies. She had Betty in bed with her. I put the babies beside her. She started cleaning them, and then she let go one of the most haunting screams or howls I had ever heard. She was crying over her dead puppies. I could tell Betty was not easy with me there, so I left Susie, the doctor, to take over. I was so shaken by Betty's soulful crying that I cried for her.

Later, Susie called me in. She had delivered four more babies, and they were alive. Betty was feeding them. I put my face to her to tell her how proud I was, and she snapped at me. Obviously, this was a lady thing, so I left Susie and Betty to the birthing. Betty had two more. The largest one died later, so end the end she had five live babies.

When I had the opportunity to examine the puppies, they did not seem deformed, but it became abundantly clear they were not bassets and were all from different fathers. Betty had obviously had a fun night out with the boys and did not discriminate.

After awhile, we recognized the puppies did have some differences from normal puppies. These deficiencies made them even greater gifts. We gave two puppies away and kept the three more gifted ones.

# Chapter 4

## Betty's Posse

*Hootie*

Hootie is blond with a white stripe down the middle of her face; her hair is as soft as a chinchilla's. She has an extra ridge of hair on her back, much like a ridgeback's. Her tail is long and curled, and her eyes are the color of a wolf's and very penetrating. Hootie has a high-pitched scream that she frequently emits. When you ask her what is wrong, she has that blank look; the lights are on, but no one is home. All of a sudden, she will just take off running until she collapses. One more unique talent Hootie has is the ability to tear holes in anything, like my sister's leather couch, the ottoman, the bed, her bed, and all her toys. Things that dogs are not supposed to be able to tear apart take just minutes for the Hootiser. A doctor's once fashionable, expensive, fine house became war zone of furniture interiors, fabric, and toy stuffing, compliments of Hootie, and she seems so proud.

## *Boogie*

Boogie is the big male of the litter. When he was formed, his head and upper body were magnificent, but his hind portion—his flanks and back legs—kind of withered in development. So he has small back legs, which are bowed. He has the coloring of a Doberman. Just to look at him from the front, you would say, "What a pretty dog!" But when he walks by, he looks like an old bowlegged cowpoke. He is a big love dog and is so sensitive you cannot yell at a football game, or he will run and hide.

## *Hummel*

What can I say about Hummel that will not infuriate my sister? It looks like Betty had sex with a baboon. Envision the same face on a dog. Add hair like a terrier's, an overbite of one and a half inches, teeth so crooked you could open cans, lips Angelina Jolie would die for, and those big monkey eyes that are always looking around. He uses his hands like a primate, and if startled, screams just like a monkey. For the longest time, until he got too big, my sister carried him around with her, and he held on to her, like one of those monkeys hanging on to Jane Goodall. The rest of his body resembles a big terrier's. My sister loves him the most, because he is so strange, but this love is shared; he has anxiety attacks when she is at work. He just waits at the back door until her arrival and gives that big monkey scream until she holds him. Now this disgusting display of emotion does not end with them hanging on to each other on the couch, he has to sleep with her with his arms around her neck. He kisses her all over her face. He thinks he can talk. When it is time to eat, he comes to me and gives me this big song and dance, which is very entertaining. I call it his monkey dance.

   Others think Hummel so ugly he is cute, but he is such a mess, only Betty and my sister could love him.

# Chapter 5

## Kyle's Chemical Kids

Now I call these babies Kyle's Chemical Kids. Kyle feels responsible for the kids being given the chemical that could have killed them. He did not know Betty was pregnant when we brought her to him, but he is such a good guy. They only see Kyle when we take them to the vet. I still like to announce on arrival, "Kyle's Chemical Kids are here!"

Betty tried to be a good mother, but these were not your typical puppies. One was climbing up the light fixtures, while another was tearing the Persian carpet apart and another was howling at who knows what. Her only means to get them under some control was the tit; they came running every time she sat down. She was raw from their constant needs or wants, but Hummel's gnarly little teeth were tearing off hunks of her flesh. Betty cleaned the little monsters as they fed, and when they pooped or peed, she would eat it, almost as if in embarrassment for her babies.

Even with the demands of her posse, she still had time for us. Betty is the best and smartest dog I have ever seen, and she is so sensitive to us. Let me explain before everyone's says, "Well, my dog …" Remember, Betty is not a retriever or large dog in stature.

She is about one foot from the ground at her highest point, and she is at least two feet wide. She has a paw span as wide a grown man's hand, with about two inches of leg to her torso. Her face has large flaps of skin, which makes it very expressive, and my god, does she show her expressions! She has a red-brown coat. Her light brown eyes, with large whites, allow the full extent of her expressions. Her tail is always going, because she is basically always happy. She wags her tail with her heart. So she is not going into a burning building to pull one of us out, and if she ran into a lake to save one of us, she would sink. She may not be a glamour dog, but she makes up for it by sheer heart and determination. She might pee on the fire, so some credit okay?

# Chapter 6

## Prissy

As I mentioned in the beginning, I was with another when I came to live with my sister. I brought my basset of many years, Prissy. She was from Peru, where bassets are renowned and heralded as the national pet. I brought Prissy back to the States with me, and she became my constant companion. She traveled with me wherever I went for work; it was a condition of my work that she travels with me, and accommodations had to be made for her in lodging. I did not trust flying her, so we drove from San Antonio, Texas, to Los Angeles, California, and back many times over a period of several years.

She loved traveling. We would make a pallet for her in the front seat, where she could sleep. We made it tall enough so that she could stand on it to look out the windows. We stayed together in dog friendly hotels up and down H-10, usually taking our time to go sightseeing and take bathroom breaks.

We were the product of a bad marriage, where Prissy was treated very badly, as was I. It felt good to be free on the road, allowing the air to blow through our hair (ears) and listening to music. When she would get tired, she would lay on her bed but always with her head on my lap.

In Los Angeles, I had a dog sitter for Prissy. They loved each other, but they fought over everything. Often, I would come home to two staunch ladies sitting in different corners, mad and waiting to tell on each other. Over the years, Tanya would take Prissy to the dog park and the dog beach, and they became fast friends and remained so until Tanya and I decided to sleep together. Prissy let her know by kicking her out of bed that there are extents to friendship and she was not sleeping with her daddy. Two years passed, and it was time for us to go back to San Antonio. It was tearjerker parting those two, but off we went.

# Chapter 7

## Back to San Antonio

I knew living with my sister was going to be a change for both Prissy and me. She had a new dog named Betty, which was going to be a distraction.

To my surprise, Betty and Prissy became good friends. Betty always led the play, licking and loving. We thought Betty would change once she had her puppies, but she actually led Prissy back to them and introduced her to the Posse. Prissy would lay with the posse to give Betty a break, but that did not last long since Prissy had no milk.

I got a new job about one hundred miles from San Antonio, so Prissy and I would get up early on Monday mornings and drive to La Grange, Texas. It was good to be on the road again. We sang along to our music. Yes, Prissy sang. She tried her best to pronounce the words. She had little success, but she thought she was cool. Her favorite song was "Shining Star," by the Manhattans. Prissy stayed in the hotel with me, but during the day, she went to a kennel. It was no Tanya, but they were good to her. In the evenings, we would get takeout food, hug on the bed, and watch TV until we went to sleep—just a man and his best friend and soul mate.

In California, Prissy had a bout with pancreatitis, caused by the takeout food I had been feeding her. They treated her with fluids and steroids. They reprimanded me and told me not to give her people food. I tried, but Prissy would go without eating rather than eat dog food. So I gave in. She had two reoccurrences in San Antonio, which resulted in the same remedy and reprimand, and the same outcome—I gave in to Prissy.

When Prissy and I came home for the weekend, my sister told me that while we were gone Betty could not be consoled. She just cried at the back door and had not eaten in three days. Our being home resolved all Betty's distress, and things were well once again.

When I was in town, I would take the dogs to this big park to run and chase the wildlife. Prissy, in particular, just loved the park. She would run until she dropped. Fun was had by the whole posse, and I had peace the rest of the day. I never missed a day at the park, because Prissy just could not get enough.

# Chapter 8

## Three to Work

It was decided that Betty would go to work with Prissy and me. Betty knew she had to be in the backseat, but I made a great bed for her. So there I was going down the street with two excited bassets with their heads out the window and ears flying everywhere. Betty just loved the adventure; she got along quite well at the kennels, and everyone would talk about how wonderful Betty was. She would not sleep in the bed because she knew that was Prissy's place. I made Betty a nice bed on the floor though.

# Chapter 9

## Prissy Has Another Flare-Up

One night, Betty woke me up by nudging me and crying. I checked to see if Prissy was next to me; she wasn't. Betty led me to a corner of the room where Prissy was all curled up, sleeping in her own vomit. It was 3:00 AM, yet the vet in La Grange came to my room. He said it probably was a flare-up of her pancreatits. He took her for the night to give her an IV with her medicine. When I picked Prissy up, she was very weak. She did not respond well to this round of treatments. At night, Prissy was more comfortable on the floor next to Betty. Betty would cry over Prissy and put her head over her body.

When we got back to San Antonio, I took Prissy to the vet, and they started new treatments. The weekend passed, and she was still sick. I supposed it would take her longer to respond. I had a short week, so I left Betty at home and Prissy at the vet.

# Chapter 10

## The End of the World

The morning after I returned to La Grange at 2:00 AM, my sister called and told me that I needed to return, right away, that they did not think Prissy would make it through the night. "*What* happened? What's wrong?" This had to be incorrect. I got back to San Antonio at 5:00 AM; the vet did not open until 7:00 AM, so I waited outside. When I entered the office, Prissy heard my voice and cried out to me. They could not restrain her. She ran out to me, and I held her shaking body. I asked, "What is this, she may die?"

They said the vet was not in yet, and he would have to explain.

"Nonsense, she is a little shaky, but she will be fine."

I took her out to put her in the car. She was too weak to get in by herself. When I got her in the car, she just lay on her bed, but her tail was going, and I smiled. I took her to the park, and she could barely get her head up to look out. She started to vomit all over the car. About that time, I got a call on my cell phone from Kyle. "Jerry, you have to bring her back. She is very sick and in great pain."

I said, "She does not seem to be all that bad."

"They will try to act well for their owners, but you have to bring her back."

As the realization dawned, a lump rose in my throat, and I could not talk.

When I got her back to the vet's, Kyle explained that the vet in La Grange had misdiagnosed her. She had advanced liver cancer. They had tried everything to combat it, but it was too aggressive at this stage.

"Well, how long does she have?"

"We need to do something soon, if you do not want her to go through any more pain."

"Please, Kyle, do not tell me this. There has to be something." At this point, it was more of a plea than a question.

"No, sorry, Jerry, there is not much more that can be done. I will go prepare what is needed. You spend time with her now." It had been years since I had felt fear, but it was back and it was crippling.

*How can I do this? I have to be strong for her.* I pulled her toward me and asked her, "What do you want me to do?"

Her eyes answered, "Take me home, Daddy, and make this hurt stop." There was such hurt and sadness in her eyes. I had always taken care of her and saved her from hurt and sorrow. She knew I would always take care of her, but now I was failing her.

She was shaking and not able to keep her legs under her. "It's time, sweetheart," I said, and she laid her head in my lap like all the times before, but this was for the last time.

As they put her down, thick, heaving sobs emanated from my very soul. The sobs were so hard I could not catch my breath; when I did, my ribs hurt from the depth of the crying. My breath was knocked out of me, like someone had punched me in the stomach. How can you live with killing your soul mate and best friend? I wanted to die. I held her sweet, tender body. The tears rolled down my face and fell onto her lifeless body. I kissed her head and tried to say, "I love you," and "Good-bye," but amidst the sobs, nothing came out. I looked up and saw that all the technicians and the doctor had tears streaming down their faces. I just sat in my car and tried to compose myself, but it was not to happen. I went home and just cried. I am haunted to this day.

# Chapter 11

## The Healing of Jerry Garton

You can cry only so much, and then you are exhausted. I was just staring off, and I saw this head bobbing up and down, just the top of the head. I realized it was Betty. Now remember, Betty has a vertical leap of a one-fourth of an inch, so she was well exceeding that. She was trying to be funny, jumping around and then running in circles. I laughed through my tears and saw that it pleased her to make me laugh.

It took days for me to get up and around. I was empty and emotionally torn apart. Betty slept at the foot of my bed, not imposing, not doing anything. She knew I needed that silliness just once, for that time. One night, I awoke to soft moans and realized it was Betty. As I approached, she started to run off. I turned on the light and looked at her, fearing she could be sick. Her face was full of tears. They ran all down her nose and mouth. She was crying; of course, I had not realized she had lost her friend also. I hugged and rocked her in my arms, telling her it would be okay. It would take time, but *we* would get over this.

So we started to heal and became regular companions. When the posse went back to the park, no one sat in Prissy's front seat, as a sign of respect.

Betty moved her sleeping arrangements from my sister's room to mine. She sleeps at the end of the bed, not in the bed, as she had with my sister. The bed was Prissy's; it was where she slept with her daddy. My sister had to reassure Betty it was all right for her to move, and then she was happy. At night, I started to look forward to her coming to bed. As I told you, she had paws the size of a man's hand, so she slid when she walked, and it was so distinctive. I heard Betty skating down the hall, and I had to smile. Her first order of business was to check on me. She did this by putting her paws on the edge of the bed, pulling herself up so her big head was resting on the bed, and looking at me through her big paws. If I was in reach, she would nudge me to see if I was awake and then kiss me good night.

This was done without expectation of remuneration. I still could not get over Prissy, but that night, I realized Prissy would want her best friend to be her successor. It hurt me that Betty had been so delicate and caring, never pushing our relationship. I called Betty into my bed; she came eagerly and laid her big body next to mine.

I washed Prissy's car bed, and the next time I went to La Grange, I invited Betty into the front seat. She was very reluctant. She was uncomfortable during our first trip but was fine after that. She had to crawl into the car because of her short legs, big paws, and rotund body. The look on her face said, "I am coming; just wait. Cool your jets," as she struggled to get into the car. I did not try to help. She would dismiss me with a snort like a pig.

# Chapter 12

## Betty Back at Work

Everyone at the hotel loved Betty. She was a charmer. She would run in circles, showing off for the staff. They all wanted her to stay at the front desk, and I had ample young ladies wanting to walk her. I still took her to the kennel daily, because they all loved her also.

I started becoming fatigued in the evenings, and it was good Betty had all the attention, but she knew when it was time to come to me. Play was fine, but her daddy was number one.

She would go to the elevator and stare at the door until one of the staff opened the door and pushed the button. Then she would make sounds at my door or scratch until I let her in.

She sleeps with her paws and arms around my arm. One night, she woke me, sniffing my mouth and crying. I tried to take her out, but that was not what she wanted. She started running around in circles crying; that was when I collapsed. Her howling brought the hotel staff, and the next thing I knew, I was in the hospital. I had heart and kidney failure.

My sister told me that Betty lay at the back door crying and waiting for me. She never left the back door or ate until I returned.

My illness prevented me from returning to work, which was better, because I could be with the posse in the day and work on projects I had neglected for years. While I thought I would be able to get work done, the posse had other ideas.

# Chapter 13

## Jerry Tries to Work from Home

My sister gets up at 6:30 AM to get ready for work, so everyone has to get up. The posse starts running through the house, barking and playing. I hear them coming and brace myself, because they run right over me. Then they come back and stand on me with their full weight. Now if that does not wake me, the kissing starts, with one on one side and one on the other so no matter which way I turn, I run into tongue. I have to get up. My awakening was heralded by the baying of hound dogs; it's like trumpeting in Caesar.

My sister puts down dry food in a bowl, which is picked up by Hummel (the chimpanzee) and dumped outside. "We are not eating this trash. How many times do I have to dump it?"

They follow my sister in to help her get ready. Now Hummel likes perfume, while Boogie likes lipstick, so she gives them both a little bit. They come out smelling and looking like two banjies. As my sister leaves, they all go to see her off at the door. She reassures them she will return but to no avail; they still have to go through the melodrama of crying and howling. This soon passes, and they come to me for their daily treat. Betty taught me by coming and talking to me then with her grunts and moans. I would follow, and she would look at the treats and jump her quarter of an inch until I gave her treats, and then all the posse came. Now unknown to me each had their own desired treat. When I put treats in front of Betty, she shook her head no and then pushed them away until I came up with the correct treat. I finally gave up and threw one of each on the floor. The look of incredulity on their faces was unbelievable; you don't throw treats on the floor. They all walked off in disgust. Boy, I had a lot to learn. My sister had spoiled these animals, and I decided, well, things were going to change. I had a book to write and e-mails to catch up on.

I got my coffee and sat at the computer. I felt them staring at me. "What do you want now?" Betty walked up and lifted my arm with her nose, so I followed her. They all went to the door. "Oh! Okay, you want to go outside?" No one went outside. Betty went to the back to the garage door and started her dance. "No! We go to the park on the weekends." They all then started their individual noises: Betty grunt talking, Hootie emitting her loud screams, Boogie howling like a hound dog, and Monkey Boy just running in circles saying something in monkey. "Okay, just this one day." Needless to say, this went on every day thereafter.

After our two hours at the park, I would be back in front of the computer. Then I would hear this loud blood-curdling scream. In the beginning, I ran to see what had happened; now I know and just take my time. Boogie, the one with the deformed body, is a bully, and he likes to tease the others. Hummel is a pansy, so Boogie loves teasing him the most. Well, when Hummel is upset, he screams— not cries, moans, or grunts—he screams a woman's scream. When I would go to see what had happened, Boogie would be looking in the air, like he was very intently counting flies. Hummel would have his toy back and would be crying over it. "Boogie, please do not tease him. You know he will cry." In spite of my admonishment Boogie never missed a day.

No sooner would I get back to the computer than Betty would want her love, which I wanted also. This is such fine ritual. It starts with kisses on her big head, the flaps on her face, and then the tummy. All the time, her tail is just saying, "I love this so much." We lay until she goes to sleep.

Then off to work I go. Once I get going on the computer, I hear fighting, so once again, I go. Hootie has gotten tired of Boogie's teasing and nipped him, so now big Boogie is all hurt. So I have to console him. Off I go once more to work. Next, Hummel is tap dancing and talking in monkey, which I do not speak, but he obviously wants me to follow. He goes to the kitchen and starts sniffing at the pots and pans and then goes to the refrigerator and looks back at me. He wants me to make their meal. This also goes on daily. Sometimes I mess with him, and when he is talking, I act like I do not understand. "What happened? Did Timmy fall down the well?"

About four o'clock, they start positioning themselves around the back door, waiting for my sister. This cannot be a simple process. Boogie pushes Betty. Betty pushes the other two, and there is more growling and crying until she comes home, and then they go ballistic.

# Chapter 14

## Checkup Time

One day, my sister informed me the dogs were due for their annual checkups, shots, toenail clips, and baths. The first to go was Betty. We entered the vet's to the chants of "Betty! Betty! Betty!" Oh, she was so excited to see her friends she ran in circles. They all ganged up around her like she had just made a touchdown. She rolled over, and they rubbed her belly. She was in heaven. I left her so she could bask in her glory.

I took Hootie next, and except for the high-pitched screams and peeing all over me, it went well, as did Boogie's visit. Hummel was a real problem. He hid under the bed. When I did get him, I had to drag him out and then carry him the rest of the way. When I got him into the vet's, he totally collapsed on the floor, peed, pooped, and starting crying, "Mommy-aaa! Mommy-eee!" They had to carry him back, and if they touched him, he would give off his monkey scream. They finished Hummel in a record time, brought him to me wrapped in a towel, and indicated I could take him home and come back to get the other dogs. I almost got the impression they did not think he was a dog. When I got him home, it was business as usual. I cleaned him up and returned for the rest of the dogs.

As Boogie and Hootie were being pulled out of the vet's, I looked as Betty was saying her farewells and noticed Betty sniffing one of the dogs that was waiting in the lobby. This was not a typical all-over sniffing but of the mouth only. I asked one of the technicians what was wrong with the dog. He told me she was dying of cancer. Betty started crying and putting her head on the dog. It occurred to me Betty knew; she knew when Prissy and I were sick too.

Every day was some rendition of the above, so the thought of being an author took a backseat to loving and caring for my cherubs.

# Chapter 15

## Then Came Little Girl

She was being prepared to be put down when I got a call from a friend of a friend. "You like bassets?"

"Yes, love them."

"Well, we have one that needs some love."

"I am on my way." I stopped and asked Susie if it was all right. She warned me about what might happen if I brought a strange dog into the posse. *It is a better chance than she has now,* I thought.

When I first saw her, my heart broke. She was tiny. I mean, she was a basset in all aspects but was miniature. Her ribs and backbone protruded from her small body.

She was blind in one eye from having been kicked, and the other eye looked like it had been kicked in also. Her back had been broken and self-healed, crooked. Her right front leg had been broken and had also healed badly. She had scabs and lumps. I gathered her in my arms and told her it would be okay.

I took her to the vet to have her checked over. She was old and in bad shape, but they said if anyone could make her last days great, it would be the Gartons.

The vet was able to research her past through a chip she had had implanted. She had had eight owners, but none wanted her. The last guy put her on a busy highway in hopes she would be hit. No matter how hard I pleaded, they would not tell me who the guy was. I guess it was for the best, because they knew that for the love of an animal, I would harm someone.

I called her, appropriately, Little Girl. Further examination revealed she had worse injuries than first suspected. She could not eat well because her mouth had been kicked in, causing the roof of her mouth to be deformed; one side was higher than the other. She hid in the laundry room, where she felt secure and warm. We did not disturb her except to give her encouraging soft words and soft food. It took awhile, but she came out of hiding to try to take a place in the family.

One day, I came home and saw her cowering in the laundry room corner, emitting little cries. She had been attacked and had massive holes in her neck. I yelled for retribution, and all I saw was assholes and elbows as they retreated. I took Little Girl to Betty and crying asked, "What happened? I know you did not do this, but one of your posse did. We do not bite in this house. I am leaving this old lady under your protection; you take care of her. I love and trust you, Betty." Betty kissed and held Little Girl in her big paws. She licked the old lady's wounds and waited until Little Girl was settled and sleeping and then softly slid off her bed and casually shuffled outside.

It was probably ten minutes later I heard a dog fight, I mean one of those with screams of pain and growls of intense anger. It did not last long but was furious. I started calling the dogs, but they all stayed in the dark. Then Betty came shuffling in, her ears all bitten and bites all over her big body. She was bleeding all over the house. When they are injured, they look much smaller. Next came the blond ditz, Hootie, crying and running in circles, as usual, and then came Monkey Boy, talking a blue streak of monkey talk. He could not contain himself, so he just fell and peed on the floor. Then came Boogie, bloodied, but head held in shame. He came to his mother and lay before her. It was sad, but Little Girl was not bitten again, and Betty was more attentive to the old lady. They were never best friends, but Betty was her protector.

The idiot dog Hummel found a friend in Little Girl. Neither is cultured in the process of dog play; they hunch over each other's backs trying to determine dominance, which neither can quite manage. But they lie in the sun together and gather warmth from each other.

Little Girl became my shadow. She just limps along beside or behind me. She is not a bed dog; she is more secure lying beside my bed at night all cuddled up in warm blankets.

On her second annual checkup, the vet discovered a huge tumor. It was cancer. He gave her a week—a month at most. He gave her steroids to make her feel better. The medicine made her happy and spry. She tries to play, acting like a puppy, but because of her trauma, she runs sideways. When I come inside, she awkwardly runs to me, with this little bark of happiness, and her broken tail just wags. She finally knows love and at the time of this writing is doing well.

# Chapter 16

## Betty's Revenge

Betty hates taking medicine, and she has done everything to make this clear. My sister and I, two doctors, thought we could outsmart her, but she seems to know every time we even move toward or think of the medicine, and she runs off. We marvel at how she knows and how dumb we look. So we have to come up with a plan of attack that rivals a ranger operation. Once, under the cover of darkness, while she was sleeping, I caught her and forced the pill down her throat, as Susie rubbed her stomach, which had a bad rash. Big mistake! *Big mistake!*

Betty gave me a look over her big shoulder of total hurt and disgust and ran away from home. Now she did not go far, just to the corner of the backyard, where she was in sight so we could get the full effect of what was to come.

She dug a hole in the ground and nested. Now it was 30 degrees and sleeting and raining nonstop. At first, it was funny, and then we became worried and made attempts to call her in. In return, we received only a hurt stare, with her big, baggy face hanging down in the mud. This went on for two days, and we knew she had to be miserable and hungry and she was going to get sick. I attempted to approach her, but she would run away and then go back to the wet hole. We put food out, but she would not eat. On the third day of this torture, I left the house to see if Susie would get better results.

When I returned, she was in the house eating but immediately ran out of the house with her tail between her legs, peering over her shoulder with this hurt look.

I finally went out into the rain and cold, sat next to her hole, and begged her forgiveness, with a promise I would not do such a thing again. She let me lead her wet, limp body into the house. She lay on a dry blanket and adjusted herself to where she was facing me with this doubtful face. I could see her body relax, as warmth overcame her. Then her eyes started to close. I guess she caught herself; seeing as the trust was not yet fully reinstated, she held one eye open, staring and watching my every move. It was macabre that she could be sleeping while that one eye followed me. Susie called it her "evil eye," and this treatment lasted a day. She stayed back in my sister's room for a couple of days. Then one day, I felt this soft nuzzling on my hand. It was Betty. I grabbed her, and we had a love fest.

It was a hard lesson for my sister and me, but it had its effect. If medicine needs to be administered, we take her to the vet. She is okay with this because she know this is the place were medicine is given. The vet says, "She has you trained well." We told him of our torture and the evil eye. He laughed so very hard saying, "That is Betty."

# Chapter 17

## Jerry's Illness

It only took one more time of Betty smelling my mouth to make me believe she knew something, so I went directly to the emergency room and found I was on the verge of another heart failure. When I am in the hospital, the posse mourns. Betty and Little Girl lie at the back door and will not move or eat. Hootie and Boogie lie on my bed. Ignuts Hummel just stares around like he has done something wrong.

I have had two more trips to the hospital, and each time, Betty knew in advance.

I just stop breathing and start gasping for breath. I am instantly suffocating. Sometimes I can get a small amount of air. Sometimes, I black out. The process repeats itself until I get to a hospital. My lungs fill with fluids because my heart cannot pump well enough, and then I slowly drown or could drown in my own fluids. The doctors convinced me I had abused my body, but I never felt that bad until it took its toll and my whole world was out of control. I cannot control any body functions. I am spinning around and around, and this makes me heave. Embarrassment soon passes because I throw up again, and again the doctors are merciful and sedate me, for the illness is too much of a stress on an otherwise fragile existence.

"Your kidneys are shot, and your heart is about useless. Its walls are paper thin. With all your existing diseases, you have no hope of living much longer. We need to keep you in the intensive care unit and monitor your condition to see if there is any possibility of prolonging your life."

Staying in the hospital was not for me. I had this panic at the thought that the posse needed me.

# Chapter 18

## The Great Escape

I noticed the staff was about to change shift—they were trying to hurry to get paperwork done and glee was in the air, with talk of the coming weekend, husbands, and girlfriends and all sorts of flirting.

I quickly pulled all my leads and the tubes in my legs and arms, got dressed, and walked down the hall to the exit. Outside, I hailed a taxi and went home to my dogs.

I was sure they were hungry, and my exit from the house in an ambulance had to have traumatized them. When I opened the front door, there was much howling, barking, screaming, and grunting as they took me to the ground under a wall of kisses. Now I felt better. I fixed their food. They gulped it down and were at the back door waiting. They wanted park time as usual. I gained strength and got in the car, and off we went.

Halfway to the park, a police officer pulled me over. He asked if I was Jerry Garton.

"Yes?"

"Sir, there are number of people looking for you. I think your sister needs to talk to you. Give her a call. I will wait."

I called her on my cell phone. "Sue, what's up?"

"Jerry! You have the medical community looking for you, as well as the police. You cannot leave the intensive care unit. You just do not do that. I told them where they would find you, with the dogs. The tubes you pulled out were in your arteries, and you could have bled out. You are under heavy sedation and should not be driving. Any stress could kill you. Your cardiologist has called me to try and find you. He says he was going to fire you as a patient. The hospital is threatening to forbid me to practice there anymore, and the insurance company has threatened to revoke your coverage."

"Okay, okay, let me meet you back at the house, so you can take me back … after a trip through the park."

"*Jerry!*" was all I heard as we drove off.

Upon reflection, I know Susie was not mad; she was laughing so hard. I broke all the rules for the dogs. She understood and would make things fine, except for the hospital staff, who tried to bully me. I had never accepted it and would not this time. I asked when all the leads were off if it registered me as dead. "How long was I dead before you discovered I was just gone?" I asked. They assigned a nurse to sit in my room until I was discharged.

# Chapter 19

## Return from the Hospital

Susie has provided as much medical home assistance as possible. She knows the torn hearts if I am not at home. Susie's intent is for me to die at home with the dogs, which makes me feel happy and secure.

Because I am wobbly when I walk, Betty has taken on the duty of nudging the back of my legs, guiding me in the correct direction. She is so smart, people.

I have a whole new perspective on life. As I look out the window and watch the dogs play with one another, it makes me reflect. This will probably be my last spring, and I am more sensitive about the passing of time. You know, Betty and her puppies may not be the best animals in the world, but their joy, love, and dedication cannot be measured. The fun and happiness they brought to my life fills my heart.

All this makes me know there has to be something good after I pass, maybe the Rainbow Bridge and Prissy. I know they all will come to me, and I cannot wait to run with them again. With all this love, I cannot fear death. I have been blessed and just want to enjoy the twilight of my life with Betty and the brats.

You cannot measure the thrill of innocent love. It is unequivocal. I guess that is why my dogs are so special, better than any other dogs, because they gave that love to me, not to anyone else.

No greater gift could be given than the simplicity of God's love, and there is no better emissary of God's love than a dog.

I do not fear dying; I feel it happening as my sundown approaches. I do not fear the pain or troughs of death. I do not fear the anguished faces of friends and family as darkness approaches. I *do* fear the last time I will look at the backyard, see Betty take her big sweet paw and smack one of her pups and then all of them start running in all directions feeling good and showing off for themselves, all cuddling around her as they bask in the warm sun—one group, one pod, one posse. So I hum an old song through tears, a broken heart, and a choked throat, "Sunshine on My Shoulders."

# Chapter 20

## Good-Bye, My Lovers;
## Good-Bye, My Friends

I want and need to say something special about my sister Susie. Since we were young, there has been a strong bond between us. I was told I never left her side. We were not only good companions; we always looked out for each other too. I knew she was hardheaded and strong willed. Once, when my brother took her place in front of the TV, she went into his drawer, got his sack of steely marbles, and clobbered him on the head, knocking him out. She was three.

Because of our parents' divorce, Susie ended up with Mother and I with our father. We drifted apart, but never was there doubt about our love for each other.

Susie is a fine physician today and looked up to by many, but none more than me. I know she had to get by in school on plain dogged determination. She was not the most gifted of students, but she made up for it in moxie. She was honors everything and a lady doctor in a man's world.

I was financially broke, healing from a broken back, and had marital problems. She insisted I come stay with her. Though I had brief periods of work, they usually ended because of my health. I will not say life was great; we had some real nasty fights, but they would always end in tears and laughter. Our love for the dogs and animals has cemented our relationship. We share them with love beyond compare. They soothe our souls and make us laugh every day.

At this time in my life, I cannot work, and if not for the grace of Susie, I would be on the street. She gives to me like a little sister, happy to make me happy. She knows my limitations and has begrudgingly accepted I am a slob and always will be. She also knows I am living on borrowed time. She has opened the house so the whole world revolves around me, and the dogs have constant access to me. I know seeing me suffering hurts her, but it is offset by the love I receive and need. She will do everything to ensure I have as many days with the dogs as possible.

I am a very fortunate man that God made my sister; she will never get the tribute due her for all the good she has done as a doctor, a daughter, a friend, and most of all, a sister to me. She is unselfish that way, and I know I cannot tell her enough how much I love her. Sadly, that's not our way.

www.ingramcontent.com/pod-product-compliance
Lightning Source LLC
Chambersburg PA
CBHW021920040426
42448CB00007B/830